THE
BEST
GIFT
ever
GIVEN

RONNIE MARTIN

Illustrated by Nathan Schroeder

HARVEST HOUSE PUBLISHERS
EUGENE, OREGON

Scripture quotations are from The ESV® Bible (The Holy Bible, English Standard Version®), copyright © 2001 by Crossway, a publishing ministry of Good News Publishers. Used by permission. All rights reserved.

Cover design by Leah Beachy

Interior design by Chad Dougherty

HARVEST KIDS is a trademark of The Hawkins Children's LLC. Harvest House Publishers, Inc., is the exclusive licensee of the trademark HARVEST KIDS.

The Best Gift Ever Given
Copyright © 2019 by Ronnie Martin
Published by Harvest House Publishers
Eugene, Oregon 97408
www.harvesthousepublishers.com

ISBN 978-0-7369-7854-5 (hardcover)

Library of Congress Cataloging-in-Publication Data

Names: Martin, Ronnie, author.
Title: The best gift ever given / Ronnie Martin ; artwork by Nathan Schroeder.
Description: Eugene : Harvest House Publishers, 2019.
Identifiers: LCCN 2019000528 (print) | LCCN 2019008567 (ebook) | ISBN
   9780736978552 (ebook) | ISBN 9780736978545 (hardcover)
Subjects: LCSH: Advent--Meditations. | Families--Religious life.
Classification: LCC BV40 (ebook) | LCC BV40 .M3825 2019 (print) | DDC
   242/.332--dc23
LC record available at https://lccn.loc.gov/2019000528

Printed in China

19 20 21 22 23 24 25 26 27 / RDS-CD / 10 9 8 7 6 5 4 3 2 1

Let the Christmas Adventure Begin!

One of the most exciting things about Christmas is the moment when you finally get to open a beautifully wrapped gift that's been sitting under the Christmas tree with your name on it. Sometimes it seems like you've been waiting for so, so long...but then Christmas Day finally arrives, and you feel as if you're almost going to burst! It's one of the greatest things ever, isn't it?

What if I told you there was an even better Christmas gift than anything sitting under your tree—in fact, better than any gift you've ever received? And what if I told you that it was given to you by the best Giver who ever was? And that the gift was so good that it could never be broken, never get lost, and never get old, but lasts forever and ever?

This is a Christmas story about many of the wonderful gifts God has given to us. It starts at the beginning of everything, when God gave us the heavens and the earth, and leads up to the most amazing, the most wonderful, the most fantastic gift of all.

All of God's gifts to us have special meaning because they come straight from His good hands and His great heart. But only one is the best gift ever given. What could it be?

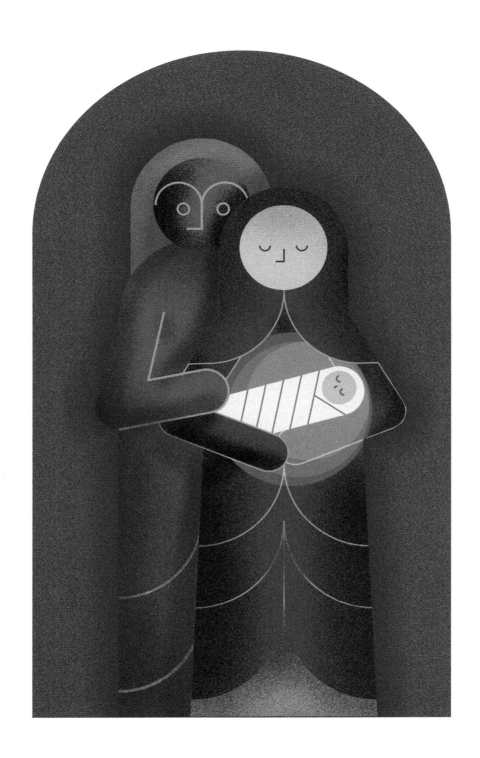

CONTENTS

God Gave Us the Heavens and the Earth

In the beginning, God created the heavens and the earth.

GENESIS 1:1

A long time ago, God created the entire universe. In it, He put a big blue sky, a bright yellow sun, a round glowing moon, and billions of bright, twinkling stars.

The universe God created is so big that nobody but God can see how far it goes. Do you know what this shows us? Just how *big* God is!

In this huge universe, God created a special place for us to live—the earth. He filled the earth with amazing things, like oceans, mountains, trees, and waterfalls. God also created all the birds, fish, and land animals. So every time you see a brown, furry bear in the forest or an owl that says *"Hoo, hoo!"* or a big whale swimming in the sea, you can remember that God created everything so that we would worship Him, give thanks to Him, and take good care of all these gifts He gave us because He loves us so much.

God's creation is a wonderful gift, but His *best* gift is even better. What could it be?

Of all the things God created, what are some of your favorites? What do they tell you about God?

Dear God,

Thank You for loving us so much that You created the universe with all the stars, the earth for us to live on, and all the beautiful oceans, mountains, and animals. We know why You gave us these good gifts—not because we deserved them, but because they show us how great and beautiful You are. Help us praise You right now and give thanks to You every time we see Your amazing creation.

Amen.

God Gave Us Good Things

God saw that it was good.

GENESIS 1:25

What are some beautiful things God created? How about the daytime so you can play and work? How about the nighttime so you can sleep while the moon lights up the sky? How about all the vegetables you pick in the garden or buy at the grocery store? How about all the apple trees and peach trees that produce yummy fruit? How about the ocean to swim in, streams to splash in, and ponds to catch fish in when you go camping with your family? How about all your friends and family and all the times you spend with them laughing, playing, eating, and worshipping God together?

After God made everything, what do you think He said? He said that it was good. Everything God makes is good because God Himself is good! So when you are outside and see a big oak tree, a furry little puppy dog, or a green grassy field to play on, you can know it is good because God made it! God has made these good things so that when we see them, we will think of Him and give Him praise. What does it mean to praise God? It means saying, "God, You are good and great and the most wonderful person in the whole world. Thank You for everything You made because all of it is so good—just like You!"

The things God made are wonderful gifts, but His *best* gift is even better. What could it be?

Why did God say everything He made is good? Why is it important to know that all good things come from God?

Dear God,

Thank You for all the good things You have given us. Please help us remember that You are even better than all of them. When some good things turn out bad, please remind us that in the beginning, You made everything good—and that someday, everything will be good again.

Amen.

God Gave Us Each Other

So God created man in his own image, in the image of God
he created him; male and female he created them.

GENESIS 1:27

After God created the entire universe, He decided to create us! He made us even more special than the animals because we are made in His own image. Imagine that! Even though we aren't God, we are *like* God in so many ways. For example, just like God, we know how to be kind, loving, patient, gentle, and caring toward other people.

How did God create us? The Bible says that out of the dust of the earth, God formed the first man who ever lived and named him Adam. He gave Adam a beautiful garden to live and work in called Eden. But Adam felt lonely because even though he named all the animals God made, none of them were just like him.

Do you know what God did? He had Adam take a nap, He took out one of Adam's ribs, and He made Adam's wife, Eve, from that rib. Adam was so happy! He thanked and praised God for Eve because now he had someone just like him to love and care for. Adam and Eve were able to serve God and worship Him together.

People are wonderful gifts from God, but His *best* gift is even better. What could it be?

In what ways are we like God—made in His image? God made Adam and Eve to help each other. How can you be helpful to the people in your life?

Dear God,

We praise You today for creating us in Your image. We are sorry we don't always treat others as kindly as You treat us. Thank You for being patient and forgiving and for helping us be more like You—the way You made us to be.

Amen.

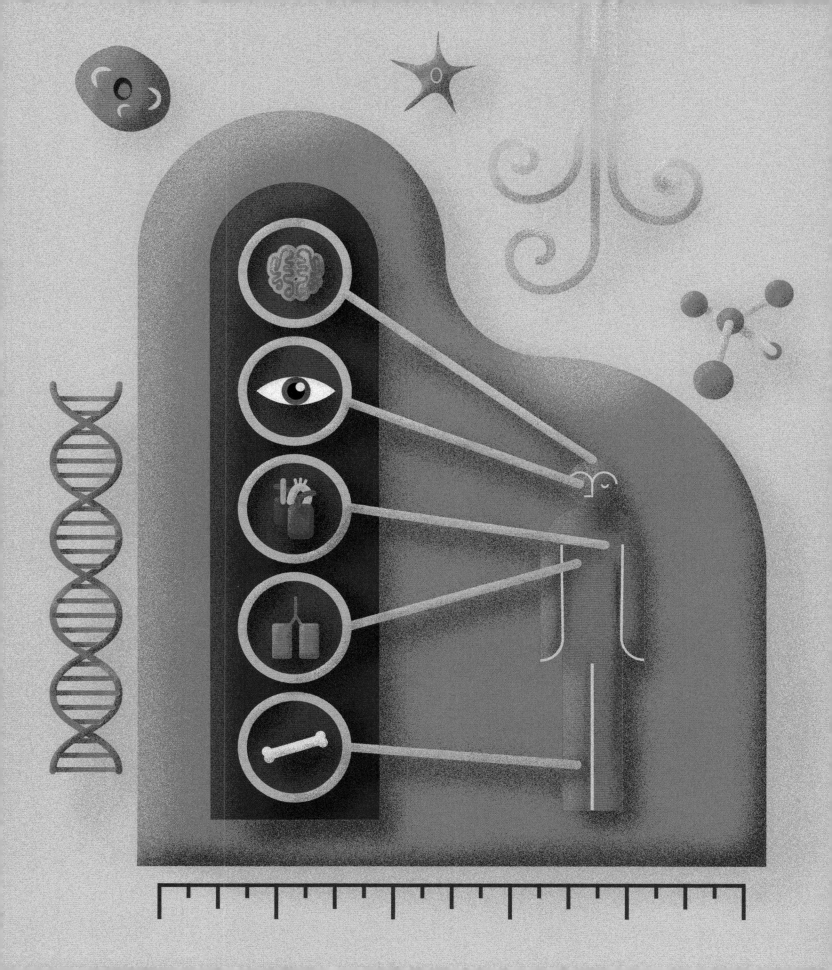

God Gave Us Rest

On the seventh day God finished his work that he had done, and he rested on the seventh day from all his work that he had done.

GENESIS 2:2

What do you think God did after He created the heavens and the earth, the daytime and the nighttime, the sun, moon, stars, animals, and people? He took a rest! God doesn't get tired like you and I do, but He rested on the seventh day to show us that resting is a good thing after we have done lots of hard work. Why is resting such a good thing? Because it allows our bodies to build up strength again so that when it's time to work, we have the energy. Rest is also good because when we're not working, we have to trust God to take care of us.

So every time you take a rest from your work, remember this: God did the same thing, and following His example is what's best for us. After you do your homework, help your brother or sister, clean your room, help your mom or dad fix something, make something special for your friend, or work hard building something, remember to take a break—just like God did. He will take care of you and renew your strength.

Rest is a wonderful gift from God, but His *best* gift is even better. What could it be?

What do you like to work on? What are some of your favorite ways to rest?

Dear God,

Thank You for giving us work to do! Work can sometimes be hard, but we know it helps us to use our heads, hearts, and hands to bless our family and others. We also thank You for giving us the rest we need. As we rest, fill our hearts with thankfulness for the work You are always doing in our hearts.

Amen.

God Gave Us a Way Out

The man and his wife hid themselves from the presence of the LORD God among the trees of the garden.

GENESIS 3:8

Something bad happened after God made Adam and Eve. He told them that they could eat from all the delicious fruit trees in the garden where they lived—except one. If they ate from this one tree, they would be disobeying God. What does disobeying God mean? It means doing whatever we want instead of doing what God has told us to do.

Your parents want you to obey them because they love you. They know that what they're asking you to do will be best for you. The same is true with God—obeying Him is good for you!

One day, a serpent came into the garden and told Eve that God wasn't telling the truth when He told them not to eat from the one tree. You know what happened? Eve believed the serpent and ate the fruit. Then she gave a piece to Adam, and he ate it too.

God knew Adam and Eve ate the fruit. He came to the garden to find them, but they were trying to hide from Him. When God found them, He told them that what they did was wrong and that as a result, someday their bodies would grow old and die. It was very bad news. But God had some good news too. He loved Adam and Eve and showed them grace. What is grace? "Grace" is the word we use when God gives us good things we don't deserve.

As bad as it was that Adam and Eve disobeyed, God was planning something that would make everything better again. But they would have to wait a long time.

Obedience is a wonderful gift from God, but His *best* gift is even better. What could it be?

What does it mean to sin against God? What should we do when we sin?

Dear God,

Just like Adam and Eve, sometimes we disobey Your commands and do what we want to do instead of doing what You want us to do. Please forgive us when we sin against You, and help us make better choices. Thank You for always loving us and for forgiving us, just like You forgave Adam and Eve.

Amen.

God Gave Us Promises

He shall bruise your head, and you shall bruise his heel.

GENESIS 3:15

Do you know what happened after Adam and Eve disobeyed God? He found them in the garden and promised them He had a plan to make everything right again. What was the plan? He promised that someday He would send His own Son to earth to make it so disobedient people could be obedient to God again. Do you know what's so great about that? When God makes a promise, He always keeps it!

All through the Bible, God makes promises to the people who love and obey Him, and He always fulfills His promises. Sometimes we break our promises to people, but God never breaks His promises to us. This is good news because it means that even if bad things are happening around us or we disobey God, we can be sure that He will still do everything He says He's going to do.

God's promises are wonderful gifts, but His *best* gift is even better. What could it be?

What are some promises you have kept? What are some of God's promises?

Dear God,

Thank You for always keeping Your promises, even when we don't keep ours. Help us remember that when things go wrong, we can trust You to make things right and to make us more like You.

Amen.

God Gave Us Grace

Noah found favor in the eyes of the LORD.

GENESIS 6:8

When God sent Adam and Eve out of the Garden of Eden, He told them to have a big family with lots of kids and lots of grandkids. But as their family grew and grew, they disobeyed God more and more. This made God very sad, so God decided to send a huge flood that would cover the whole earth.

One of Adam and Eve's grandsons was named Noah. God showed grace to Noah (God shows us grace by giving us good things even though we don't deserve them). He told Noah to build a big boat called an ark so that Noah, his family, and many animals would be saved from the flood.

Noah obeyed God and built a big ark, just as God asked him to. It took him a long time to build it! When it was all done, God told him to take two of each kind of animal into the ark with him. Can you imagine all those animals walking into the ark? Lions, bears, monkeys, elephants, giraffes, zebras...think of all the noise they would have made!

After Noah and his family and all the animals were in the ark, God shut the door and sent a big storm that covered the whole earth with water! But Noah, his family, and the animals stayed safe and warm in the ark because God made sure nothing happened to them. Why did God do this? It was because God loved Noah and wanted to save Noah from the flood.

The ark was a wonderful gift from God, but His *best* gift is even better. What could it be?

How has God shown His grace to you? How can we show grace to others?

Dear God,

Thank You for giving us grace and showing us favor—just like You did to Noah and his family and all the animals in the ark. Please forgive me when I think I'm strong enough and good enough to do everything on my own. I know that's not true. Instead, everything good that happens to me is because of Your grace. Thank You for giving me all the good things I don't deserve. Please help me be more thankful every day.

Amen.

God Gave Us a Home

The LORD said to Abram, "Go from your country and your kindred and your father's house to the land that I will show you."

GENESIS 12:1

One of Noah's great-great-grandsons was named Abram. One day, God told Abram to pack his bags and leave his home because God had a new home for him, far away in a new land. God loved Abram and chose him to be the father of a great nation that would someday be the people of God.

So Abram obeyed God, packed up all his things, and started his long, difficult journey. Abram didn't even know exactly where God wanted him to go, but he trusted God the whole way, and God led Abram to the land He promised to give him.

When Abram and his wife Sarai were very old, God gave them a new baby, whom they named Isaac. God changed Abram's name to Abraham, and He changed Sarai's name to Sarah. Abraham and his family explored their new land until he was very old. When Abraham died, he gave everything he had to his son Isaac.

Our homes are wonderful gifts from God, but His *best* gift is even better. What could it be?

Does moving to a new city and a new home sound scary, or does it sound fun? Have you ever done something that at first seemed big and scary but then worked out okay?

Dear God,

Thank You for preparing a new home for us in heaven. Please help us trust You during our journey here on earth—even if we don't always know where our next home might be.

Amen.

God Gave Us Families

Your offspring shall be like the dust of the earth.

GENESIS 28:14

Abraham's son Isaac married Rebekah, and they had twin sons named Jacob and Esau. Jacob got in trouble one day because he pretended to be his brother Esau and tricked his father into giving the family's blessing to him instead of Esau! Esau was so mad, Jacob was afraid and ran away to live with his uncle.

What Jacob did was wrong, but God took care of Jacob. All the promises God had made to his grandpa Abraham, He now made to Jacob. Jacob got married and had twelve sons and a daughter.

How big is your family? Maybe you have lots of brothers and sisters, or maybe it's just you. Did you know you have more than one family? God gives us another family—a big one!—called the church. Every week when you go to church, you can see lots of your brothers and sisters. God gives us a big church family so we can learn how to love and serve Jesus.

Our families are wonderful gifts from God, but His *best* gift is even better. What could it be?

Why do you think God gave us families to live with? What are some ways you and your family members can help each other?

Dear God,

Thank You for brothers and sisters, aunts and uncles, teachers and friends. I pray that You will help me be kind to them—to treat them all as family. Thank You for including me in Your family!

Amen.

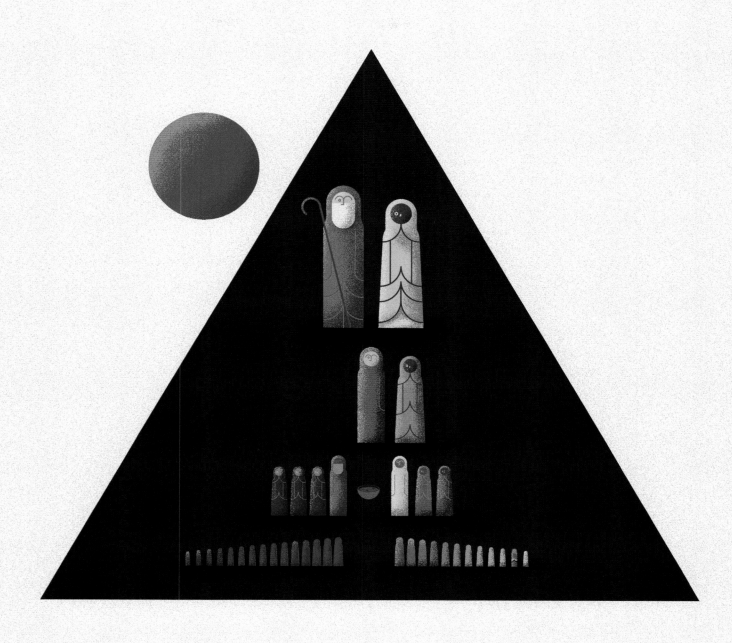

God Gave Us Help

God meant it for good.

GENESIS 50:20

The Bible promises that God is always ready to help us. But sometimes He doesn't change our difficult situations right away. This is what happened to a young man named Joseph.

Joseph was the favorite son of his father, Jacob. In fact, Jacob loved Joseph so much that he made a special coat for Joseph, but he didn't make one for any of his other sons. Joseph's brothers were jealous. They were also mad because Joseph told them he dreamed he would rule over them someday. They decided to get rid of Joseph, so they sold him as a slave, and he was taken to a faraway land called Egypt.

Joseph had a hard life in Egypt and spent many years working long hours for men who weren't very kind to him. He was even put in prison although he hadn't done anything wrong! But God never stopped protecting Joseph and helping him through all the hard days.

One day, a man called Pharaoh, the ruler over Egypt, had a dream. Nobody could tell him what the dream meant—that is, nobody but Joseph. He told Pharaoh that a famine was coming. Then he told Pharaoh that if the people saved part of their food now, they would have enough to survive when the famine came.

Pharaoh was so happy, he took Joseph out of prison and put him in charge of all of Egypt!

One day, Joseph's brothers came to Egypt to ask for food and were shocked to find out that their brother Joseph had become a ruler.

Do you think Joseph was mad at his brothers for all the bad things they did to him before? No, Joseph forgave them because he knew that God had used all those bad experiences to save people. This is what God does in our lives. When bad things happen, He helps us through them and uses them to accomplish something good.

God's help is a wonderful gift, but His *best* gift is even better. What could it be?

What are some ways God has helped you? What should we remember when God doesn't seem to be helping us?

Dear God,

Thank You for always helping Your people, even when things don't appear to get better right away. When bad things happen to us and we don't understand why, help us remember that You haven't forgotten us. As Joseph had faith in You, may we trust You to help us through difficult times.

Amen.

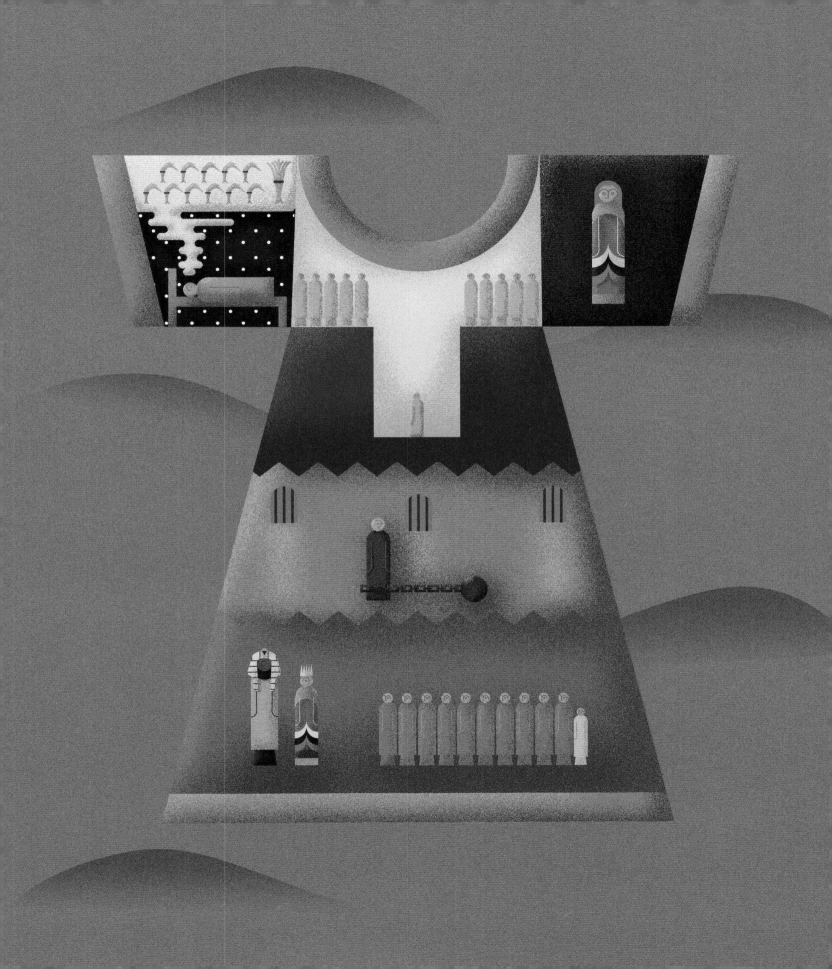

God Gave Us His Laws

If you will indeed obey my voice and keep my covenant,
you shall be my treasured possession among all peoples.

EXODUS 19:5

The Old Testament contains an important story about a man named Moses. One day, God came to Moses and told him the time had come for His people to leave the land of Egypt. God promised to lead His people through the desert to a new home where they would enjoy many wonderful things. God gave His people laws so they would know how to live good lives and be happy. God wrote His laws on two big stone tablets and gave them to Moses on top of a great mountain. The first and most important law was that the people should worship God alone.

But when Moses came back down the mountain, he saw that God's people had broken the first law. They were worshipping a golden statue of a cow, pretending it was another god! What do you think happened?

The people were afraid when they saw Moses because they knew that worshipping a statue was wrong. They stopped worshipping the golden cow and told God they were sorry. And you know what? God forgave them. He showed them mercy by not giving them the punishment they deserved.

We don't always obey God's laws either. But God will forgive us when we tell Him we're sorry and make better choices.

God's laws are wonderful gifts, but His *best* gift is even better. What could it be?

Why do you think God wants us to obey His laws? What should we do when we break God's laws?

Dear God,

Thank You for giving us such good laws to obey. We know that You give them to us because You love us and treasure us and want us to love and treasure You. Please forgive me for the ways I didn't obey You today, and help me make good choices tomorrow. Thank You for loving me and for showing me so much mercy every day.

Amen.

God Gave Us Hope

Blessed be the LORD, who has not left you this day without a redeemer, and may his name be renowned in Israel!

RUTH 4:14

There was once a girl named Ruth who had to leave her home and travel a long way to a place she'd never been before. Ruth was probably afraid, but she put her hope in God to help her. When Ruth arrived at her new home, she found a job working in the fields picking grain. God gave her enough grain every day so that she and her family had enough food to eat.

God also gave Ruth a special friend named Boaz. Boaz was a very good man who owned a big field and let Ruth pick all the food her family needed. Ruth wasn't afraid anymore because God had helped her all along the way and given her hope.

What does it mean to put your hope in God? It means believing God will do good things even when things around you seem very bad. Ruth put her hope in God because she believed He would take care of her even when she didn't know how He would.

What do you think happened to Ruth and Boaz? They fell in love, got married, and had a baby! It was a special baby too, because their baby would someday become the father of King David.

Hope is a wonderful gift from God, but His *best* gift is even better. What could it be?

What is something you hope will happen? What does God want us to do when we are afraid of what might happen?

Dear God,

Even when we can't see what's going to happen, we can have hope in You. You will always work things out for good for those who love You and are called according to Your purpose.

Amen.

God Gave Us Courage

Who knows whether you have not come to the kingdom for such a time as this?

ESTHER 4:14

The Bible tells us the story of a young Jewish woman named Esther.

One day, all of the most beautiful women in the land were brought into the palace of the king because he was looking for a new queen. Esther was one of the women, and when the king saw her, he chose her to be his queen. But Esther had a secret—she was Jewish, and some of the people who worked for the king didn't like the Jewish people.

One day, an evil man named Haman came up with a plan to get rid of all the Jewish people. Esther's cousin heard about the plan and asked Esther to go to the king for help. But the king had made a rule that no one could come talk with him unless they were invited—not even his queen. If someone came to see the king without an invitation, he held out his scepter if they were accepted. If he didn't hold out his scepter, they were punished.

Esther's cousin told Esther that maybe the reason God made her the queen was so she could help save God's people from the evil Haman. Queen Esther had to make a decision. Would she be brave enough to approach the king without an invitation and ask him to save God's people? Or would she be too scared?

Esther decided to ask the king to help—and he did! And God saved His people through Esther's courage, even though she was so afraid.

Courage is a wonderful gift from God, but His *best* gift is even better. What could it be?

What is courage? When have you needed God to give you courage?

Dear God,

Sometimes when things get scary, we want to run the other way. Today we ask You to give us courage to face scary things because we know we can trust You and You are always by our side. Help us remember that since You are with us, You will always give us the courage we need when we ask You for it.

Amen.

God Gave Us Forgiveness

With you there is forgiveness, that you may be feared.

PSALM 130:4

King David was Israel's mightiest king. David loved God and did everything God told him to do. And when David disobeyed God, he asked God to forgive him. God loved King David and called David a man after His own heart.

How do we ask God to forgive us? We tell Him that we're sorry and that we want to make better choices from now on.

One time, King David disobeyed God very badly. Here is how it happened.

David had a brave soldier named Uriah. Uriah was married to a beautiful woman named Bathsheba. One day, when Uriah was away fighting with the army, King David took Bathsheba away from her house and made her his own wife. This made God very sad. So what did God do?

He sent Nathan the prophet to visit David. Nathan told David the story of a farmer who owned just one little lamb that he loved very much. Now, the farmer had a neighbor who had many lambs, but one day, his neighbor stole the one little lamb from the farmer and his family.

When David heard the story, he became so angry! He said he was going to punish the man who stole the little lamb! But the prophet Nathan reminded David that just as the man had stolen the little lamb, David had stolen Uriah's wife.

David was ashamed because he knew Nathan the prophet was right.

What did David do? He asked God for forgiveness—and God forgave him, just like He forgives us when we tell Him we're sorry and that we want to make better choices.

Forgiveness is a wonderful gift from God, but His *best* gift is even better. What could it be?

What does it mean to sin? What should we do when we sin?

Dear God,

Thank You for forgiving us when we tell You we are sorry and that we want to make better choices. Please show us when we make poor choices, like Nathan did for David, so we can come to You and make things right. God, please help me want to do things that are pleasing to You, like being kind to my friends, obeying my parents, working hard at school, and spending time praying and reading my Bible. Thank You for always loving me.

Amen.

God Gave Us Prayer

O God, hear my prayer; give ear to the words of my mouth.

PSALM 54:2

King David was not only a mighty warrior and king but also wrote many prayers and many songs of worship to God that we pray and sing in church today. What does it mean to pray? It means to have a conversation with God. We can tell God how great and wonderful He is, confess our sins to Him like David did, and thank Him for being such a good God who shows us grace and mercy.

We can also ask God for things we need. Sometimes we need God to give us things like food, help, clothing, or a place to live. We also need God to fill our hearts with love, joy, peace, patience, and self-control. God wants us to ask for those things too.

God loves to hear us pray, and He listens carefully to everything we say to Him. When we pray, God does some wonderful things in our hearts. He reminds us how much we need Him and how much He loves us. He helps us think about our choices, and He always forgives us when we ask Him to. Prayer helps us remember that God is watching over us, that He has given us many good things, and that He is with us even when bad things happen.

No wonder David prayed so much! The more we talk with someone, the more we get to know them. The same is true with God—the more we talk to Him, the more we get to know Him and remember how well He knows us!

Prayer is a wonderful gift from God, but His *best* gift is even better. What could it be?

What are some things you can pray for? What are some things you can thank God for?

Dear God,

These are some things I love about You...
These are some things I'm sorry for...
These are some things I'm thankful for...
These are some things I need...

Amen.

God Gave Us Songs

Oh sing to the LORD a new song; sing to the LORD, all the earth!

PSALM 96:1

King David was a musician. He loved to play his harp, write songs, and sing them to God. David used his favorite songs to praise and worship God.

God made people to worship Him, just like David did. When we worship God, we tell Him that He is the most awesome, most wonderful, most important person in the universe. When we do that, God puts joy in our hearts and reminds us of His love for us.

At Christmastime, we can sing lots of songs to praise and worship God. "Away in a Manger," "Silent Night," "Joy to the World," and "Hark! the Herald Angels Sing" are all songs that give praise to God at Christmastime.

What other songs do you like to sing to praise and worship God? Sometimes when we are a little sad or we're having a bad day, singing to God can help. Praising God with songs can remind us that God will never leave us and that we can trust Him to take care of us.

Music is a wonderful gift from God, but His *best* gift is even better. What could it be?

What are some of your favorite songs to sing to God?

Dear God,

Thank You for giving us Psalms, an entire book of the Bible filled with songs of praise to You. We know that You love hearing Your people sing, so help us sing to You with all our hearts. You are a great God who loves us, cares for us, and shows us so much grace and mercy. Let the words we sing to You give us joy and gladness for all that You are!

Amen.

God Gave Us Wisdom

How much better to get wisdom than gold!
To get understanding is to be chosen rather than silver.

PROVERBS 16:16

The Bible tells the story of King Solomon, who was the wisest man who had ever lived. Do you know how he became so wise?

One night, God appeared to King Solomon in a dream and told Solomon that He would give him whatever he asked for! Can you imagine that? Solomon didn't ask for lots of money or a new house. Instead, he asked God for wisdom so that he could rule his kingdom the way God wanted him to.

What is wisdom? It's learning the things God has told us in the Bible, believing them, and putting them into practice. It's trusting that everything God says is good and true! It's believing that God is even better than all our favorite things because He is the one who gave them to us.

God gave King Solomon great wisdom—and He also gave Solomon great wealth! So Solomon built a magnificent temple to God and a big palace for him and his family. He also bought ships that sailed across the sea and many horses—almost too many to count! But Solomon knew the most important thing in the world was God.

We can ask God for wisdom just like King Solomon did. God will give us wisdom as we read His words in the Bible and obey them. Loving God more than anything else in the world is the wisest thing we can do.

Wisdom is a wonderful gift from God, but His *best* gift is even better. What could it be?

. . . .

What are some of your favorite things in the world? How can you enjoy them wisely?

Dear God,

Thank You for being wiser than everyone else in the world. Lord, as I hear Your words, please share Your wisdom with me. Help me love You more than all the nice things You have given me, and show me how to make good decisions that please You in everything I do.

Amen.

God Gave Us Prophets

All Israel from Dan to Beersheba knew that Samuel was established as a prophet of the LORD.

1 SAMUEL 3:20

A long time ago, God asked certain women and men to go before all the people and speak His words to them. These women and men were called prophets.

Samuel was one of God's prophets. One of Samuel's jobs was to go to the people and say, "Don't forget about God! Remember how much He loves you! Make sure you love Him and obey His words!" Samuel had another job too. When God chose a new king, Samuel made the announcement to all the people. God used Samuel to introduce Israel's first two kings: King Saul and King David.

Do we have prophets like Samuel today? Not exactly, but when we go to church and Sunday school, God gives us people who teach us God's Word just like Samuel did. They carefully study the Bible and help us learn what God says. If you see your pastor or Sunday school teacher this week, say thank you to them for teaching you God's Word!

Teachers are wonderful gifts from God, but His *best* gift is even better. What could it be?

Who are some of your favorite teachers or pastors? What is one important thing they taught you recently from God's Word?

Dear Lord,

Thanks for the all the teachers and pastors who work so hard to teach us so many good things. We pray that You will help them study and be good learners so they can teach us to be good learners of Your Word.

Amen.

God Gave Us Prophecies

The Lord himself will give you a sign. Behold, the virgin shall conceive and bear a son, and shall call his name Immanuel.

ISAIAH 7:14

Isaiah was one of God's greatest prophets. Isaiah told the people everything God wanted him to, and then he wrote down God's words so nobody would forget them.

The words Isaiah spoke were called prophecies. What are prophecies? They are God's words to the people. In some prophecies, God tells us what is true and right. In other prophecies, God tells us about the future. One of the prophecies Isaiah spoke was about a special baby God would send to us so He could be with us. The baby's name would be Immanuel, which means "God with us."

The people who lived in Isaiah's time would never get to see this special baby that God told Isaiah would be born someday, so they had to trust that God was going to keep His promise.

When we read about God's prophecies in the Bible, we learn that when God says something will happen, it happens!

Prophecies are wonderful gifts from God, but His *best* gift is even better. What could it be?

Why is it important for us to believe God's Word? Do you think God could ever tell a lie?

Dear God,

We thank You for all the prophecies You wrote in the Bible—the ones that have already come to pass and the ones that haven't yet been fulfilled. We know that You never lie and that everything You have said will come to pass. Help us remember that You are always faithful and that You have a wonderful plan for the world!

Amen.

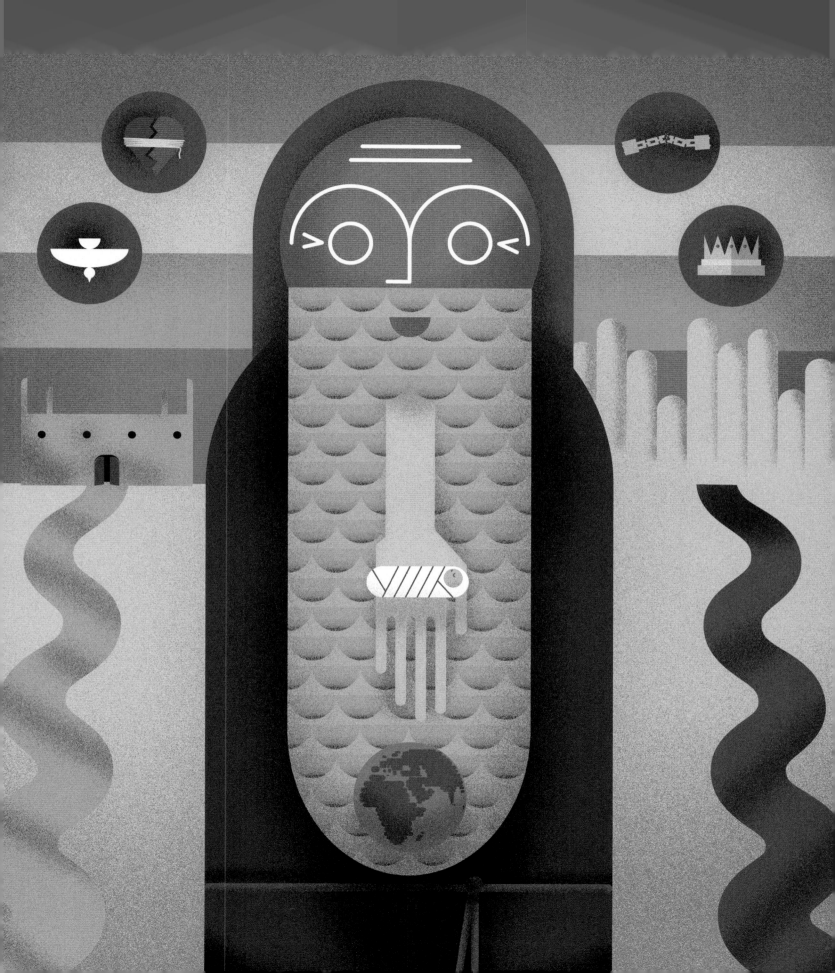

God Gave Us John the Baptist

You will have joy and gladness, and many will rejoice at his birth, for he will be great before the Lord.

LUKE 1:14-15

There once was a man named Zechariah who was a priest. He was married to a woman named Elizabeth. Zechariah and Elizabeth loved each other and loved God very much.

Zechariah and Elizabeth had never had a baby of their own, and sometimes that made them sad. But one day, an angel visited Zechariah and told him that he and Elizabeth were going to finally have a son and that they should name him John. The angel also said John would be a special baby because he would prepare the way for Jesus, God's own Son, to come.

What would John do to prepare the way? He would tell everybody about God's Son and why God sent His Son to the world—to save the world from sin.

When Zechariah heard what the angel had to say, he wasn't so sure the angel's words would be fulfilled. He didn't think he and Elizabeth could have a baby anymore because they were too old. But the angel, who was named Gabriel, told them that God would make it so. And because Zechariah didn't believe God, he would not be able to talk until baby John was born! Can you imagine what it would be like to not talk for all that time?

Everything came to pass just as the angel said it would. When John was finally born, Zechariah wrote his name on a piece of paper so all his friends and family knew what to call him. As soon as he did that, he could talk again! The first thing Zechariah did was bless God!

John the Baptist was a gift from God, but His *best* gift is even better. What could it be?

What are some ways we can tell other people about Jesus like John the Baptist did?

Dear God,

We thank You for sending John the Baptist to prepare the way for Your Son. Please help us be more like John the Baptist and tell people about You and all the great things You have done, like sending Your Son to us. Help us be bold and have courage when it comes time to tell people about our love for You.

Amen.

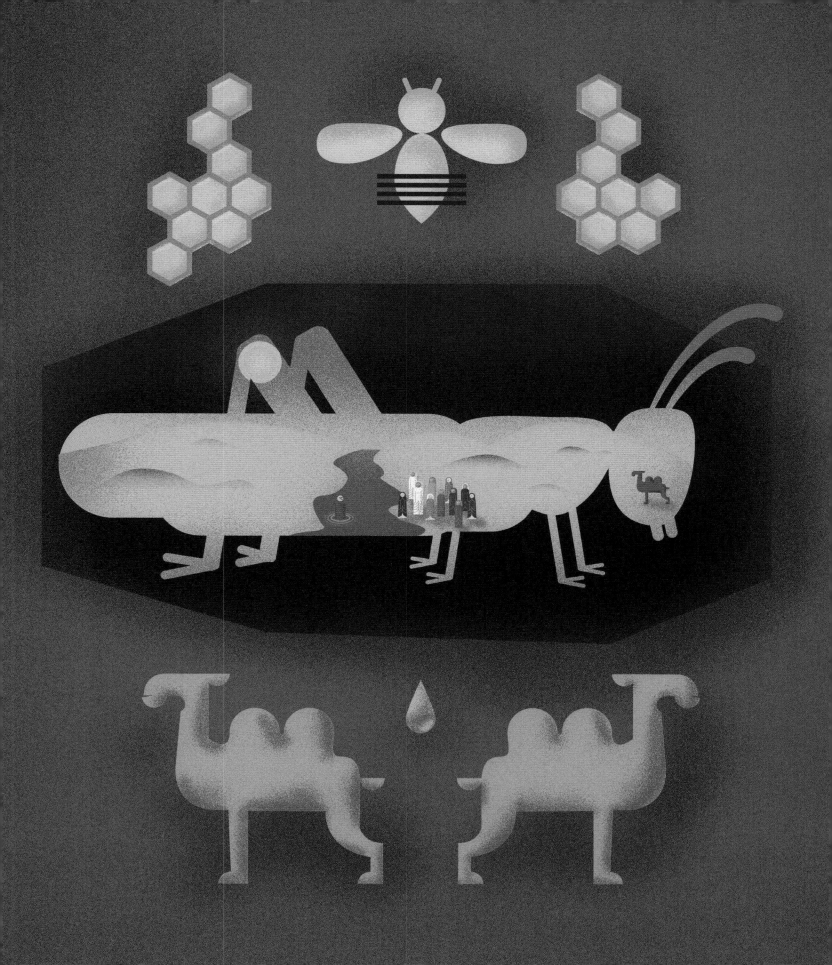

God Gave Us Mary

The angel said to her, "Do not be afraid, Mary,
for you have found favor with God."

LUKE 1:30

There once was a young girl named Mary, who was engaged to be married to a man named Joseph. Mary didn't know it at the time, but God had a very special plan for her.

One night, an angel of the Lord visited Mary and told her something wonderful. He told her she was going to have a baby! But it wasn't going to be just *any* baby; this baby was the most special baby ever born. The baby's name would be Immanuel (which means "God with us").

Why was this baby so special? Because He was the Son of God. God had chosen Mary to carry His Son, whom God sent from heaven to be with us.

Mary was very afraid when she saw the angel, but she said she would obey everything God said. God knew it wouldn't be easy for Mary, but He loved her very much, just like He loves us and helps us when He asks us to do hard things.

Mary was a gift from God, but His *best* gift is even better. What could it be?

Why do you think Mary was afraid when she saw the angel? Have you ever been afraid to do something God wanted you to do, but you did it anyway?

Dear God,

Thank You for letting Mary be the mother of Your Son. We know that it was very hard for Mary to obey You, but she did it anyway. Please help us obey You when we have to do hard things too.

Amen.

God Gave Us Joseph

An angel of the Lord appeared to him in a dream, saying, "Joseph, son of David, do not fear to take Mary as your wife, for that which is conceived in her is from the Holy Spirit."

MATTHEW 1:20

There was once a man named Joseph, who was engaged to be married to Mary. He was a very good man who loved God. He was also a skilled carpenter who made many beautiful things out of wood.

One day, Joseph was visited by an angel, just like Mary was, and the angel told him not to be afraid because Mary was going to give birth to God's Son. Joseph had an important job to do. He needed to take care of Mary and help her when God's Son was born. And that's just what he did.

When it was almost time for Mary to have the baby, she had to travel with Joseph to the town of Bethlehem, far away. Joseph made sure Mary was safe and warm on their long journey. When they arrived, they were sad to learn that there was no place for them to stay. What would they do?

They would have to sleep in a stable with all the animals. There were probably sheep and goats in the stable—and maybe even a kitty cat or two! But God kept them safe and warm as they waited for His Son to arrive.

Joseph was a gift from God, but His *best* gift is even better. What could it be?

. . . .

How have you helped someone? What are some ways that God helps us?

Dear Lord,

Thank You for sending Joseph to help Mary so that Your baby Son was kept safe. Please help us look for people around us who need our help so we can help them like Joseph helped Mary. Thank You for helping us whenever we ask You to.

Amen.

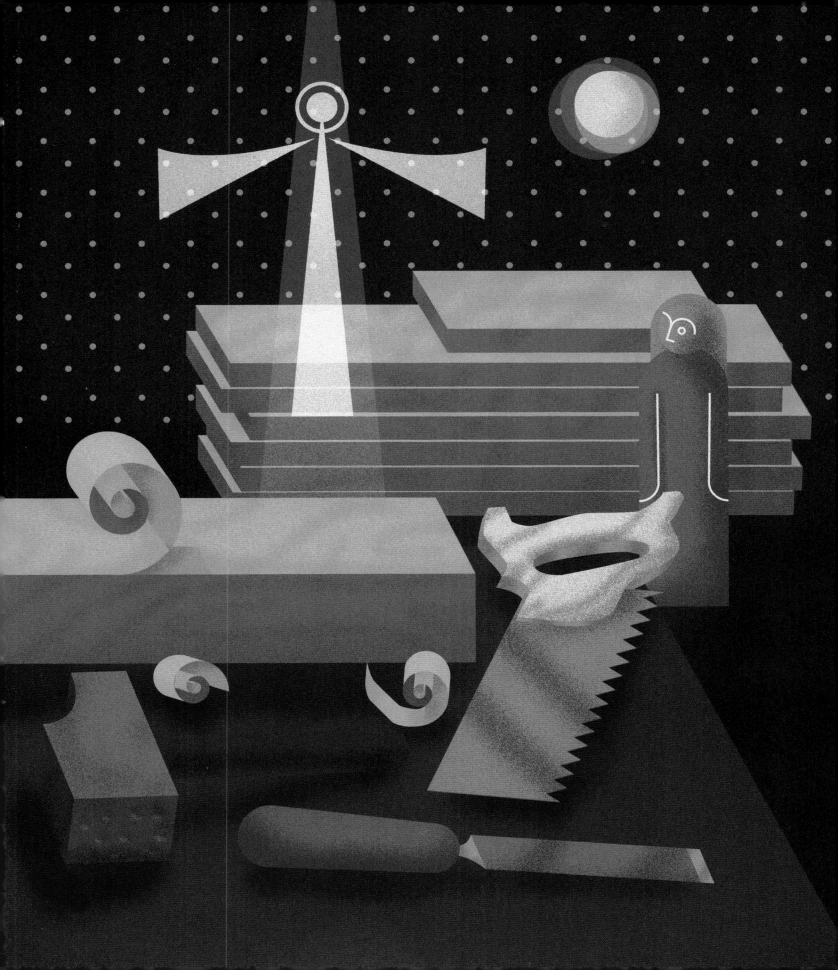

God Gave Us the Shepherds

The shepherds returned, glorifying and praising God for all they had heard and seen, as it had been told them.

LUKE 2:20

Joseph and Mary waited for God's Son to be born in the stable in Bethlehem. Meanwhile, in the fields close by, some shepherds watched over their sheep.

Suddenly an angel appeared to them in the night sky and told them he had good news for them. He told them that a special baby was born in Bethlehem—a baby that would be the Savior of the whole world.

But where would they find this baby? The angel told them the baby would be wrapped in swaddling cloths and lying in a manger. The shepherds were so excited! But before they could leave to find the baby, a multitude of angels suddenly appeared in the sky, praising God and singing, "Glory to God in the highest, and on earth peace among those with whom He is pleased!"

The shepherds ran as fast as they could to Bethlehem, and when they arrived, they saw Mary, Joseph, and God's special baby lying in the manger, just like the angel said. They were so excited, they went through the town and told everyone what they saw!

These shepherds' message was a gift from God, but His *best* gift is even better. What could it be?

Have you ever told anyone about God? Who are some people you could tell? What could you say?

Dear God,

Thank You for telling the shepherds about the birth of Your special baby. Help us be brave like them and tell people how great You are and how You sent Your Son to be our Savior.

Amen.

God Gave Us the Angels

Fear not, for behold, I bring you good news of great joy that will be for all the people. For unto you is born this day in the city of David a Savior, who is Christ the Lord.

LUKE 2:10-11

The Bible tells us that sometimes, God sends His angels to visit us. Who are angels? Angels are God's messengers that He sends to earth because He has an important message that some people need to hear.

God doesn't send angels very often, but when He did in the Bible, people were usually very afraid. Does that mean angels are scary? No, it just means that the angels looked very different from us and that they had been sent by God Himself.

Sometimes angels had good messages, and sometimes they came to warn people. When angels appeared to the shepherds near Bethlehem, they shared the best news ever: God's Son, the Savior of the whole world, was born in Bethlehem! When the shepherds heard this good news, they praised and glorified God. Then they ran to Bethlehem to see for themselves!

The angels' message was a gift from God, but His *best* gift is even better. What could it be?

When has somebody given you good news? Have you ever shared good news with someone?

Dear God,

Thank You for sending the angels to the shepherds to announce Your good news. We know this message wasn't just for them but for us too. Help us tell others about the good news of God's Son, just as the angels shared it with the shepherds.

Amen.

God Gave Us Jesus

She will bear a son, and you shall call his name Jesus,
for he will save his people from their sins.

MATTHEW 1:21

Joseph and Mary traveled a long way on their journey to Bethlehem. When they arrived, they were very tired, but there were no rooms left in the town for them to stay in. The only place they could find was a stable filled with animals.

When nighttime arrived, everything became quiet, the moon and stars were twinkling above, and the animals were fast asleep. And then...guess what happened? Mary had her baby! This was not just any baby—it was God's special Son, and they named Him Jesus, just as the angel told them to.

God's special baby wasn't just for Mary and Joseph. God sent His Son for all of us because He loves us. Jesus would grow up to teach the people about God and show everyone what God was like. Then He would die on a cross so God could forgive us for our sins when we ask Him to. God sent Jesus to die for us so that someday, when He makes everything in the world right again, we can be with Him forever and ever.

God has given us many good gifts because He's a good Father. But one gift is the best of all.

Jesus gave Himself to us so that we could have peace with God and someday live forever with Him in heaven. How can we have peace with God? By telling Jesus we're sorry for our sins, thanking Him for dying on the cross, and spending the rest of our lives learning about Jesus, obeying Jesus, and loving Jesus more and more until we see Him someday in heaven.

God has given us many good gifts, but Jesus is the *best* gift ever given!

What are some of your favorite Christmas gifts? Why is Jesus even better than your favorite Christmas gift?

Dear Jesus,

Thank You for being the best gift ever given! Thank You for coming all the way to earth to show us what God is like and die on the cross as our Savior. Help us learn from You and live for You for the rest of our lives. Even when we do something wrong, we can ask for forgiveness and You will forgive us! Jesus, of all the gifts we have, You are the best gift.

Amen.